Iceland
Laugavegur Trail
Stephen Platt

www.leveretpublishing.com

Iceland: Laugavegur Trail
First published - July 2017
Published by
Leveret Publishing
56 Covent Garden, Cambridge, CB1 2HR, UK

ISBN 978-0-9957680-9-3

Iceland
Laugavegur Trail

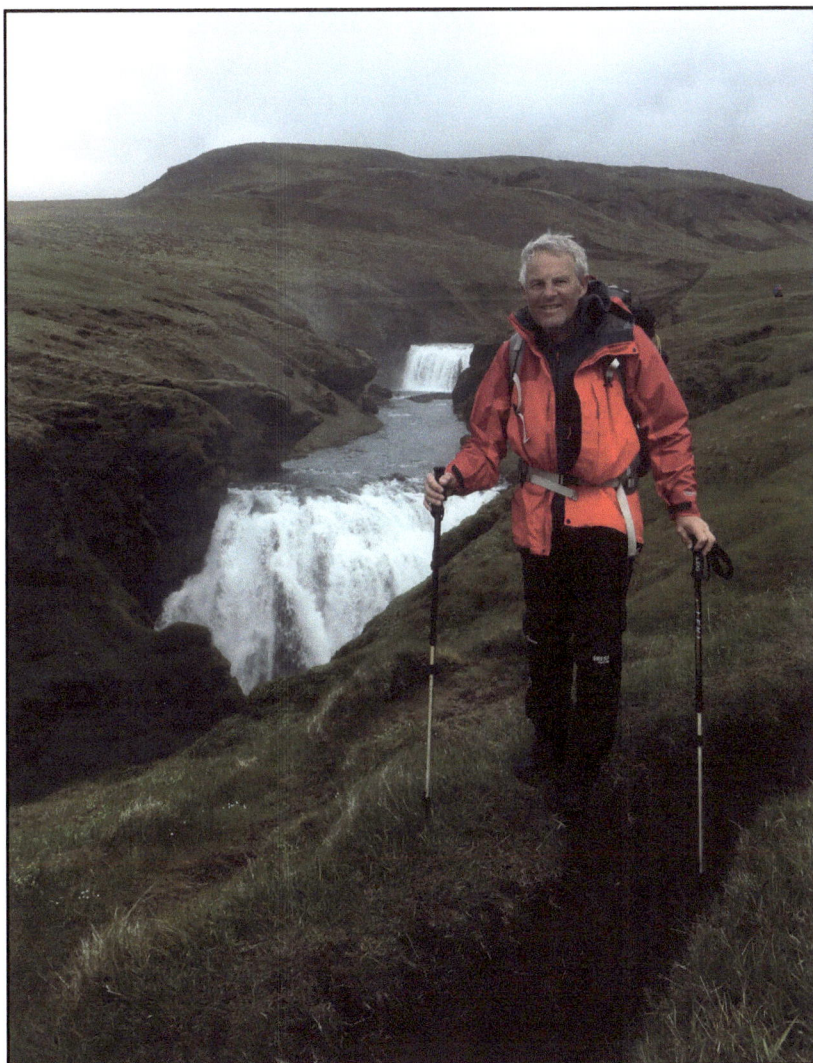

Iceland 2017

Landmannalaugar - Skógar

Akureyri
Egilstaðir
Reykjavík
Keflavík
Landmannalaugar
Þórsmörk
Skógar

Til/to Jökulheimar
F228
F229
Veiðivötn
Sveinstindur+
Krókslón
F225
Landmannahellir
Dómadalsleið
Landmannaleið
208
32
Þjórsá
26
Hekla
Kraka-tindur
Rauðu-fossa-fjöll
Landmanna-laugar+
+Höll
F208
Eldgjá
268
Reykjadalir
Laufa-fell
Klofs-fjöll
Kalda-klofs-
+Hrafntinnusker
Torfa-jökull
Hólaskjól+
Álftavatnskrókur+
Skyggnisvatn
Skaftá
Fjallabak syðra
Miðvegur
F210
Tindfjalla-jökull
+Álftavatn
+Hvanngil
Strútsskáli+
Hólmsárlón
F210
Botnaleðar
261
Fljótshlíð
Þverá
Markarfljót
F249
Þórsmörk
F261
+Hattfellsgil
+Botnar-Emstrur
Mælifellssandur
Húsadalur, RE
Skagfjörðs-
skáli FÍ
+Básar
tivist
+Fimm-
vörðuháls
Eyjafjalla-jökull
Mýrdalsjökull
F232
Hólmsá
Tungufljót
210
1
Fjallaskálar
Mountain Huts
©Landmælingar Íslands
+Skógar
Blautakvísl
Til/to Vík
Skýringar
Legend
+ Skáli/Mt hut
Hafursey
Mýrdalssandur

Reykjavik

Sunday 11 June
I caught a late flight from Gatwick that arrived in Reykjavik at midnight to bright sunlight. The sun set as we drove through lava fields into town. There was a tiring walk from the bus station, dragging my heavy suitcase. I found my apartment with the help of blonde girl who I met in the street. Got to bed at 2pm and it was still light as day.

Monday 12 June
I walked east to the University. There views down to the sea. It is a bright sunny day and since many of the papers are over my head I spend most of the day sitting outside in the sunshine. My paper is mid-afternoon and it goes okay and I get some good questions. There is a reception and I stock up on hors d'oeuvres and wine. That evening I walked back into town and found a supermarket to buy milk and then just catch the Grey Line travel agency before they close at 8pm and find out about tours to the Golden Circle.

Golden Circle

Tuesday 13 June
I book my ticket for 10.30 and visit the Stay Safe people in the city hall. They are the mountain rescue people and they show me photographs of the Hrafntinnusker hut deep in snow and explain that this early in the season the road to Landmannalaugar at the start of the walk is still closed. I plan to do the four-day trail from here south to Þórsmörk (Thorsmork), but it seems this will not be possible. So I think about changing plans and going straight to Þórsmörk, which is much lower, camp there and do day walks.

I find a nice place for coffee while I wait for my pickup. The driver is a chatty Swiss girl who tells us she loves Iceland because the people are so positive. A couple ask her how people cope in the long dark winter. She says it's hard. Some go to Spain for two or three months. It's cheaper and some people have holiday homes, she says. And everyone drinks fish oil every day, which is rich in Omega three and vitamin D. I can't stand it, she says.

Hallgrímskirkja, modern 'cathedral', Reykjarvick

   She drops us at the Grey Line bus station and we climb aboard our minibus and set off for Thingvellir where the continental plates of America and Eurasia are pulling apart and have created a deep rift. It is famous as the site of one of the first parliaments anywhere. There is a broad walk into the gorge and there are lots of tourists. The weather is fantastic with clear views of the surrounding

Þingvellir, rift valley where the American and Eurasian plates ate pulling apart

mountains and long vistas to the east. From my vantage point on the edge of the gorge one can look across the green valley basin with its church and scattered homesteads.

Our young guide is informative. He studied geology at Edinburgh University

Site of Alþingi (Althing) Icelandic parliament founded 930

and is very knowledgeable. On the way here he tells us that Iceland was settled by Norsemen in 870 and the whole island was settled in sixty years. Thingvellir is the site of the Athling, the Icelandic parliament, which met here every year from 930 till 1789.

He tells us about Halldór Laxness, the Icelandic Nobel Prize winner, and his book Independent People, which is about life in Iceland in the 13th Century. It sounds grim. He says people made shoes out of fish skins. It sounds fishy. He says Iceland only has a population of 300,000 people and two thirds live in the capital or surrounding area. He is half Italian and half Icelandic and seems very proud of his country, especially their care of the environment. Explains how they use geothermal energy to district heat the capital and how they are self-sufficient in electricity having only to import oil for vehicles. He says he expects them to move to all electric vehicles very quickly. I'm surprised they haven't made the change already. He says the parliament met for two weeks each summer to make laws, adjudicate disputes and punish offenders. Men were beheaded or hung and the women were drowned in a small pool.

I cover a lot of ground. We only have half an hour – this is an express tour;

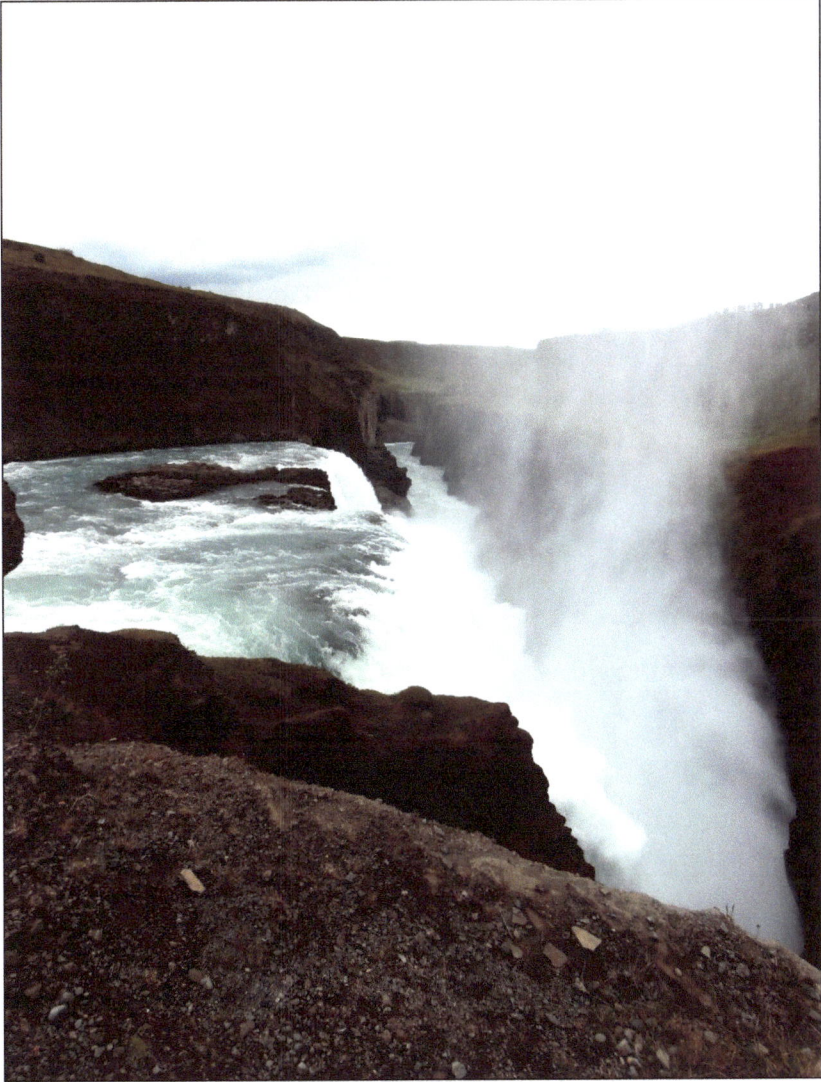

Gullfoss falls saved by Sigriður Tómasdóttir who campaigne to prevent hydro electric dam

I have to be back by five to go to the conference dinner. Nevertheless I watch a swan fly along the valley and swoop low over the lake and land beautifully next week its mate.

Next stop is the Gullfoss falls. Again we learn a little of its history. This land was owned by a farmer who sold the rights to an English hydro company. They would have drowned the falls in a reservoir. But the daughter of a neighbour objected. She and her younger siblings had been guiding early tourists to the falls. She devoted her life to campaigning to overturn the concession and was finally successful.

There is a broad walk that drops steeply from the parking and suddenly one sees the falls below the column of mist. The falls are spectacular. Two sets of falls plunge into a deep and narrow canyon, which a sign tells me, sometimes overflows. I walked to the end, passing through a section where the mist falls as rain.

I stood overlooking the first drop, watching the huge volume of water pouring over the rocks. It is tempting, like the feeling one gets standing on the edge of a cliff and imagining one can fly, to imagine being carried by the tremendous flow and being hurled into the depths of the gorge, wondering what might be one's chance of surviving.

On the way back I deviated from the path into the tundra and lay in the sun looking up at the sky. The grass and moss was soft under me and lying

Bench outside Gullfoss coffee shop

down I could watch the small flies rather than being bothered by them. I got back to the restaurant next the parking and sat on a rustic bench. I must have misjudged the time because our young guide came to find me.

Our final stop was Geysir were a 35m geyser pouts every few minutes. Apparently we get the word geyser from the Old Norse meaning to rush. A

Strokkur and Geysir, first geysers known in Europe. Used to reach 170m, now 30-40m

English geologist first documented the phenomenon in the 19th Century and adopted the name.

I sat on a bench watching for the blast, but people kept stopping in front of me so I moved on. Stupidly I took a photograph of myself rather than the geyser on my first attempt having pressed the reverse image button on my iPhone. Eventually I got a good photo and, having watched water boiling in various pools, I headed back to the bus.

I nodded off on the way back on the bus and woke as we cross the spiky lava fields. Our guide explains how it takes 200 years for moss to cover new lava and much longer for scrub vegetation to appear. He told us how people came out collecting blueberries in summer. He said he also collected porcini mushrooms. They grow tomatoes, fruit and vegetables in geo-thermally heated and artificially lit greenhouses. Iceland was once covered in forest but the early settlers cut the trees for boats, houses and fuel. Now they are planting trees – North American Aspen, native birch and Norwegian pine. They have also introduced Alpine lupins from Alaska in the 19th Century and the hills around are covered in swathes of purple. I read later that these are a pest and are killing off the more delicate native vegetation.

I got back, changed and walked to the restaurant. I met my friend Polat and his wife from Turkey was introduced to a Ph.D. student called Pinar from The technical university in Istanbul. We talked outside and then sat together over dinner. She told me her husband was an emergency medic and they both wanted to move to Germany. She said her people came from eastern Turkey and were very traditional. It was a relief it was to be somewhere where your gender wasn't an issue. She had done her Masters in Japan and felt she had never been accepted as a structural engineer there. We talked about Brexit, Syrian refugees, Armenian genocide and my trip to Van, researching recovery after the earthquake. She asked if I'd been to Northern Turkey and I said I would like to go.

Polat made a lovely speech about Ragnar, in whose honour the conference had been organised. Pinar and I walked down to the seafront and sat by the water chatting and then parted company and I got to bed.

Wednesday 14 June

I spent the morning packing and going to the bus station to book my bus to the mountains. I have been in a dilemma trying to decide whether to stick to my original plan of a four-day trek or to cut my losses and go straight to Þórsmörk. I rang the warden for the latest advice and a nice woman advised me that the next hut would be open and that, with luck, I should be able to reach it. So I went to the bus station stopping for a coffee of the way and booked. From there I walked to the University. I'm doing a lot of walking. I cut through the park and then sit outside the auditorium until coffee time.

The KnowRisk teams from Italy and Portugal, who I have been working with, pitched up at lunchtime and I sat in on their sessions all afternoon and gave my paper.

At coffee I talked with Bjarni Bessason, a Professor of Civil Engineering at the University of Iceland. He had done the trail and I asked his advice. He thought it was early in the year and that there would be a lot of snow. If it wasn't too windy I should make it to Þórsmörk.

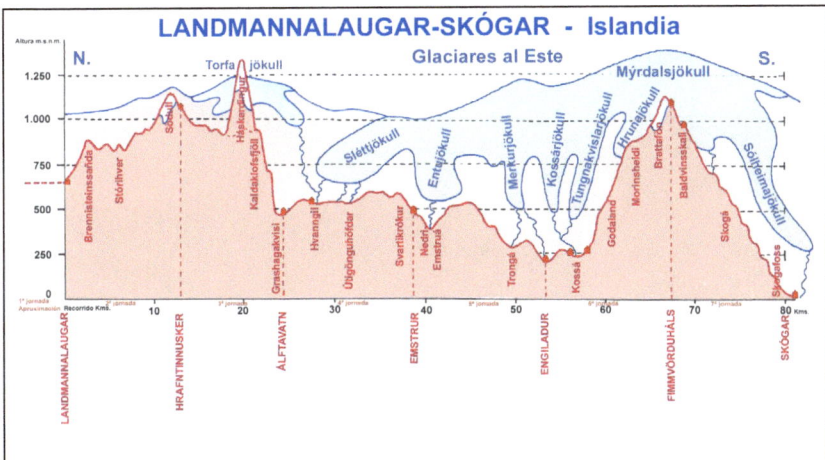

Laugavegur Trail up and downs. Thorsmork to the Fimmvörðuháls Pass looked toughest.

Landmannalaugar Hrafntinnusker Álftavatn

Thursday 15 June

There are so many sights and so many emotions in a long day in the mountains, yet nothing much happens apart from your steps across the landscape. I'm in my tent after supper. It's been a great day. I woke at five and got ready. I had planned to walk to the City Hostel, where the bus started, but suddenly I baulked at starting the day with a 3km walk. So I rang for a taxi, which came at 6am. It was chilly waiting and I chatted to a French couple who are going on the same trek and to an American couple. They had been visiting cousins in Rawtenstall in Lancashire and had also been on the Golden Circle tour. We don't usually go on guided tours, the woman said sweetly.

The bus was a large coach. It was empty at first but we picked up walkers at various places en-route including Selfoss, where a couple boarded. He was upset because his ticket said single but he insisted he had paid for a return.

Starting out from the Lanndmannalaugar hut

The driver said that he'd check on no problem. The man turned to me and said would I move. It would be nice to sit at the front for a better view, he said. Are you together, he said, referring to Austrian girl in the other front seat. I am happy here, I said. You're happy there, he said sarcastically. Can I sit next to you then. Sure I said moving my anorak from the seat next to the window. He huffed loudly, having expected I would shunt over, and sat next the Austrian girl where he could stretch his legs ostentatiously. We stopped for a loo break and I bought coffee and a delicious flapjack of oats and raisins.

We left the hardtop and drove 4 miles down a narrow dirt road. It was the sort of road one might take gingerly in a 4x4. But the young driver took it in style, fording a deep stream as we approached Landmannalaugar.

I checked in with a nice woman in the information office and I left my name. I fixed my gaiters and set off. There were other couples en-route – the French pair from the bus, a Finnish pair and a couple of Americans. They were ahead of me at first, but because they stopped more often I overtook them and stayed ahead all day.

Lanndmannalaugar valley

Scenes from the first day climbing Brennisteins

Starting out from the Lanndmannalaugar hut

The trail climbs through ash-fields covered in sparse moss and intermittent patches of snow. The patches get bigger until, about halfway to the hut, the snow becomes continuous. There were some steep sections. I contoured up efficiently but even the gently rising parts were most tiring since one broke through the crust or stumbled in other people's steps.

I stop for lunch at a cairn and get out my apple, Parmesan cheese and nuts and raisins. The Finns caught me up and I asked them to take my picture. There was a little mist that obscured the highest peaks but the weather was gloriously fine.

I plodded on, getting tired and deciding that it was the right decision to stop at the hut and not overdo it. I got there finally at 3pm. It had taken me 4 hours to do the 12 km, which I thought was pretty good.

I found a place at a crowded table in the sunshine and had a slice of the sour-dough loaf that I had brought from the Portuguese bakery in Cambridge. Half an hour later the sun was still shining and I thought why not go on. It's the same again to the next hut and I can camp near the lake. So I shouldered my pack and set off.

Hrafntinnusker hut in deep snow

A young lad shot past me, asking if I was alone and saying that solo was the best way to travel. It was longer on the snow than I expected, and most tiring. At one point I missed the main path following some steps it felt wrong. I couldn't see anyone ahead but looking back I could still see the last huge cairn. So I reasoned that the main trail must be to my left and I struck off in that direction. The snow was deep and there were faint signs of crevasses. Rather stupidly I tried to cross one and plunged in to my waist. I hauled myself out, cursing myself as a fool and skirted round and found the path. There were great views of Háskerðingur and other surrounding mountains, and fumaroles and bubbling streams were the glacial melt water was boiling.

Finally the trail climbed to the rim of the ancient caldera and the air cleared and the snow became more intermittent. It was a steep descent and tricky with loose stones like ball bearings. I was overtaken by an English couple. He had a tripod and stopped to take photographs. I was ahead again when I came to a stream which I forded. But again it seemed wrong even though there was a good path. I looked around and could see posts on the trail on the other side of a wide river. So I went back and ran into the couple with a tripod.

Climbing rim of Torfajökull caldera

Descent from the Jökultungur

We were wondering how to cross the fast flowing stream when a young lad jinked across. The man waded in using his tripod to steady himself. I took off my pack but my wading slippers were at the bottom of my rucksack. So I girdled my loins and waded in. I felt the water top my boobs despite the gaiters and cursed. I stopped and took off my socks and rung them out and continued.

It was still another 3km but I finally I made it and found a soft green spot for the tent. The warden was helpful, charging my phone and looking up times for buses from Skógar in case I decided to go all the way having gained a day by doing two stages in one. I made dinner, washed, texted Scharlie, wrote my journal and got to bed.

Álftavatn to Emstrur

Friday 16 June

I woke a few times in the night, but then slept fairly deeply to 7.30. I woke in a rush feeling it was getting late and that I needed to get going. I had dreamt I was being smothered and found a guy rope had come loose in the night. The wind was stronger and there was rain in the air, so I took the tent up to the washhouse shelter and packed it there.

I was the first away and others were just emerging from their tents. It started raining immediately. The trail was obvious and climbed and then traversed, dropping to a fast flowing river where I had to strip off my trousers and put on the rubber shoes I'd brought. The flow was fast and I stumbled once but I got across and dressed and set off again. It was much greyer than yesterday and I wondered if it would clear.

I dropped down to the Hvanngil hut. It was sheltered here between

Camp at Álftavatn hut

stone walls and people were camping and a young couple were about to set out. The caught up with me up as I was contemplating how to cross the Brátthalskvisl River. It looked serious. I shouted to the couple to ask if they would like to cross together. They came over and we stripped off. I suggested, since the boy was strongest, that he went first. He chose a place just below a line of rocks. I had thought about here and rejected the idea since I thought the water would be deeper. But he thought they would break the current. I didn't object. He stepped in holding his girlfriend's arm and I followed. It wasn't so bad. Water came up to our mid-thighs, but I was more careful than on the previous crossing and we all reach the far side safely.

This was the start of a huge ash field that extended for miles. It was tedious trudging through the fine ash and sand. The first part followed a roadway and at some point I realised there were no more footprints and no holes from walking poles. I had been daydreaming and had missed the way. I looked around. I could see the bridge I needed to cross and decided to stay on the road even though it was further. The road curved round I could see the couple

Kaldaklofskvisl River crossed by a bridge. Joy!

way to my left on the brow of an ash-black hill. We met again at the river. They were prospecting a place to cross upstream, but it seemed okay where I was. I could see a line of stones and taking care not to slip I crossed without getting my socks wet.

What does one think about when one is walking alone? At one level it's tiring and painful. Feet, legs, back and shoulders hurt. At my age you are continually monitoring your body and weighing up how you're doing and if you'll make it. You are also keeping a look out for marker poles and cairns and observing the spoor of previous walkers footsteps and the small holes their walking poles. At another level walking a long distance alone is a kind of yoga, a kind of therapy. There is an internal dialogue that is never silent of course, one aspect of which is trying to learn to pronounce the name of the next hut and the previous huts correctly. Occasionally you stop; your attention is caught by the sound of a bird or a view and for a moment you truly appreciate the immensity of where you are and its beauty. But you get your camera out to capture the moment and the feeling is lost.

Bristol couple stripping off to cross the BratthEalskvisl River.

I crossed the wooden bridge and soon after the trail diverged from the road. The next few kilometres were fairly brutal. I have been wondering about giving the next hut a miss and going on to Þórsmörk but my hips felt wobbly and it seemed hard enough just to get to Emstrur, the next hut.

I stopped at some rocks, the only feature, apart from distant surrounding peaks, in the expanse of ash. There must have been a fairly recent eruption since the vegetation was only beginning to take hold in tiny scattered patches. I had some cheese, but since I was stiffening up I set off again. I saw the young couple from Bristol at the same rocks I'd stopped at.

It was another 3 km to Emstrur. It seemed longer but finally I was there. I was undecided what to do, so I stopped and unpacked my tent from the top of my pack climbed down to the stream below the huts and checked out the various plots. There were quite a number of available flat sites but they were all bare earth and sharp stones. So I went in search of a flat vegetated site and finally found one next to the stream above the other tents. It was cramped but I thought it would do. I pitched the tiny tent, taking care to fix new guy

Stórkonufell Pass; coming to the end of the ashfield

ropes from cord I had brought with me and using rocks I plucked from the stream as anchors.

I climbed back to the hut and was alarmed to see that my rucksack and poles were gone. I couldn't believe anyone would take them so I went to see if the warden had moved them inside. He knew nothing about it and came to look with me. I had been looking outside the wrong hut and my sack was still where I'd left it outside the hut further along. What a relief. I went and played my camping fees and asked for a receipt. The woman asked me to write my name and then said, Oh Stephen Platt you weren't supposed to be here until Sunday. The woman in Landmannalaugar had rung through. I asked about the phone signal and she said I could climb the neighbouring hill. She could also offered to send Scharlie an email saying I was fine.

I made lunch of bread, cheese and apple and the woman came over and asked if I was cold. She said campers weren't usually allowed in the hut but I was welcome to go in with the Italians and get warm. The Bristol couple arrived and we chatted until they went off to pitch their tent. I gathered my things and went into the hut to write my journal in relative warmth.

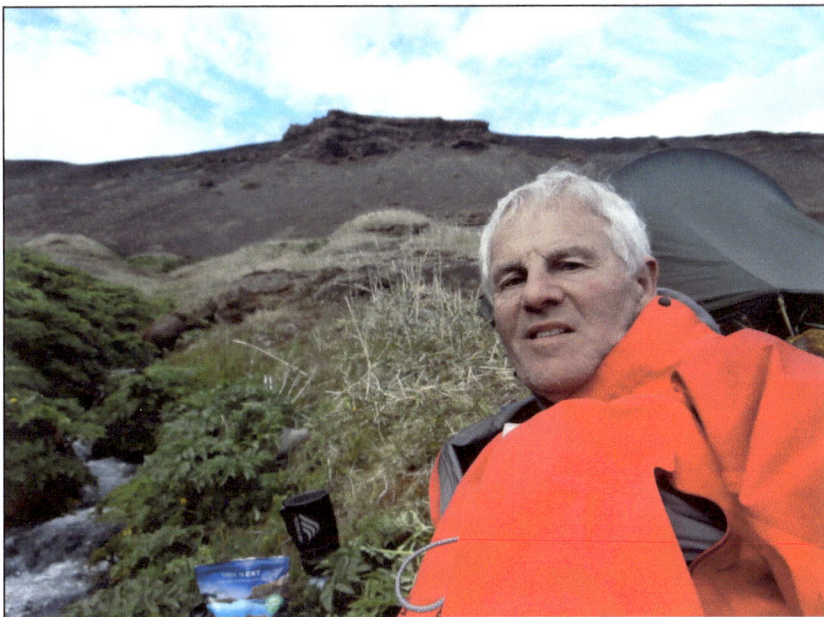

Campsite at Emstrur on a tiny flat patch of grass between two streams

Emstrur to Fimmvörðuháls Pass

Saturday 17 June

I woke at five. It was raining, but if I wanted to have any chance of getting to Skógar I would need to get going, so I packed in the tent and carried it over to the wash room where there was a porch where I could fold it.

I set off at six; no one else was about. It was drizzling but I had my full rain gear, which was just as well since he came on to rain heavily. It is hard to remember the route even just 12 hours later. But the first part dropped down to a deep chasm where there was a bridge over a dramatic drop and then an airy traverse. It was a long way, 15 km to Þórsmörk. Finally I got down to tree line – sweet smelling stunted trees with tiny birch like leaves. I found out later that these were in fact called Sweet Birch (Betula Lenta). And birdsong. Not just the haunting piping of the open country but real song.

I passed three lots of people camping near streams, still asleep in their 4-season tents. Mine, weighing in at a little over 900gm, only just survived

Markarfljót Canyon

Bridge across Markarfljót Canyon

the night and the top of my sleeping bag was a little wet, probably from condensation on the inner tent since the flysheet had kept out the water that are pooled on the roof. I would have liked a better shelter but I would not like to carry it.

There was a horn shaped mountain in the mist, the huge Mÿrdalsjökull glacier to the east and a deep canyon that I crossed by a bridge. Again the sense of vertigo looking down was unnerving. People are being up here playing in four-wheel-drive vehicles and had gone off-piste, damaging the fragile cover.

Finally I reached the wide Þröngá River with its gravel bars. Normally one can get across from by hopping from one gravel ridge to another. But today the river is swollen with heavy rain and melt water and much too deep to jump across in boots, so I disrobe. The flow was strong and came to my knees but I made it safely except that halfway across a dozen young riders on the stout Mongolian horses emerged from the trees and waded across a hundred yards down from me, all looking askance at me in my underwear.

Finally I reached a sign: to the right the Volcano hut, restaurant, and bar, to the left the Langidalur and Basar huts. It was only midday so I figured that,

Gravel bars on the Þröngá River too deep to ford in boots

after a good rest, I might have a crack at continuing, so I turned left. The last kilometres into Þórsmörk was through sweet smelling scrub. Wild flowers were just emerging from winter and I had been hearing peeping song all the way. Now there was lots of birdsong. Later in Reykjavik, in a park, I saw a Redshank piping the same cry. I'd also heard a grouse like bird that I took to be Ptarmigan and saw the black-and-white flash as it shot away. Nearing the refuge in Þórsmörk (Thorsmork) I saw a bird size of a thrush with the redbreast perched on a pole with an insect in its mouth.

No one was around at the hut so I got some water to make a brew. A young man said I could use the empty shop to rest rather than sit out in the rain so I moved my stuff. I made tea and a cheese sandwich and had a rest.

The weather had cleared so I decided not to wear my waterproof trousers since I would be climbing – a mistake. I had watched young men fooling around with a huge Mitsubishi four-wheel pick-up, driving into the river and motoring up and down. Now it was my turn to try and cross. I walked upstream a kilometre until I reached two temporary bridges and made my way to the Basar hut. It was all very touristy but a young man I asked said it

Langidalur hut, Þórsmörk (Thorsmork)

was 12km to the Fimmvörðuháls hut but 800m of ascent. It didn't seem so bad, so I set off in good spirits.

The path was steep with steps in places. There was a delightfully airy ridge and I was enjoying myself looking down into the deep valleys either side. Then it got more serious. I could see the way up the steep hillside with a traverse to a coll. It was hard and I was pleased to make it thinking, that's the hard bit done. Little did I know.

There was a long flat area of stones ejected from the last eruption and on the other side a drop down to a pass and then a long steep snow slope. I asked for directions of four lads coming the other way. Yes, it's the snow slope, they said, see where we slid down. It was gruelling – snow alternating with ash. I finally made it, having traversed to the left.

The tall yellow marker poles are very reassuring when you're on your own. Again I thought I'd made it, but the snow was only just beginning. There was another summit to climb and then more up and downs. I stopped a couple of women for advice. She had a GPS and said she had been walking in the Highlands for decades but had missed the upper hut in the mist. Worrying.

Kattahryggur narrow ridge in the Útigönguhöfði (Abode of the Gods)

Don't worry you can't miss the lower hut, just follow the poles, best of luck, she said

It was tiring and had begun to rain heavily. I couldn't stop to put on my waterproof trousers as I couldn't take off my boots easily. I should have put them on earlier before the first snow slope when I stopped for a quick rest and some chocolate and put on my anorak. My trousers were getting really wet. Never mind, I thought I can dry them in the hot, if I can only find it.

It seemed interminable and I just had to keep plodding on, hoping the hut would be over the next rise. I had assumed the hut would be lower down, below the snow line, but I'd come to realise I was wrong. I should have done my homework better. Finally I saw the peak of an A-frame roof in the mist. It was still a trudge up a snow slope but finally I was there. No signal though, so I can't tell Scharlie I'm safe.

I unpacked my way things and made drinks. I couldn't face my dry meal and didn't much feel like food. So I wrote my journal in front of the fire in my steaming trousers and finally got to bed about 9.30.

I chatted to the warden, a young man with a beard. I complimented him on

Fimmvörðuháls hut seen through the mist

his English. I said it had been a long day and I was glad of the reassurance of the marker poles even though in the UK there are no markers of any kind. I decided to sleep on the pile of mattresses in the corner of the downstairs room rather than disturb everyone upstairs. But they woke after I had been in bed a while to make drinks; luckily they were quiet.

Fimmvörðuháls Pass to Skógar

Sunday 18 June

I woke at 5am, dressed and made tea and muesli and set off at 6. The warden had told me it would take four hours so I had plenty of time to get my bus at 4.30. It was still misty when I left the hut but a break in the cloud allowed me a glimpse of the first hut on top of the ridge.

It was 15km to the coast but it didn't seem too bad. My legs were feeling fairly good and although the pack seemed heavy I knew I'd make it. There was still a lot of snow at first, but the way was clear. After a kilometre or so the path

Leaving the Fimmvörðuháls hut in the early morning

joined the Skógar River and followed it all the way down. There had been an emergency shelter earlier in the snow where the roadway that reach the hut diverged from the path; but it was locked. I lost track of how many wonderful falls I passed, stopping to take photographs at each of them. Sometimes I had to go near the edge and was conscious that one false step and I would tumble down the cliffs of the deep canyon and into the torrent and be swept away. It created a sense of anxiety. I crossed a rickety bridge over the chasm and followed the path on the other bank.

The canyon became really dramatic – a deep green cleft with white Arctic Terns circling in the updraft. Birds were nesting on tiny ledges on the steep cliffs. Maybe it was the unattached males who are showing off.

After a 3 hours people passed me climbing up. Nearly all were couples heading out at the start of the walk. Later, as I neared Skógar, there were lots of day-trippers coming up to see the first falls. One offered to take my photo. Finally there was a long steel staircase with a viewing platform of the first falls and then I was down.

I went for coffee and found out about the bus. I rang Scharlie to tell her I

One of many falls on Skogá River

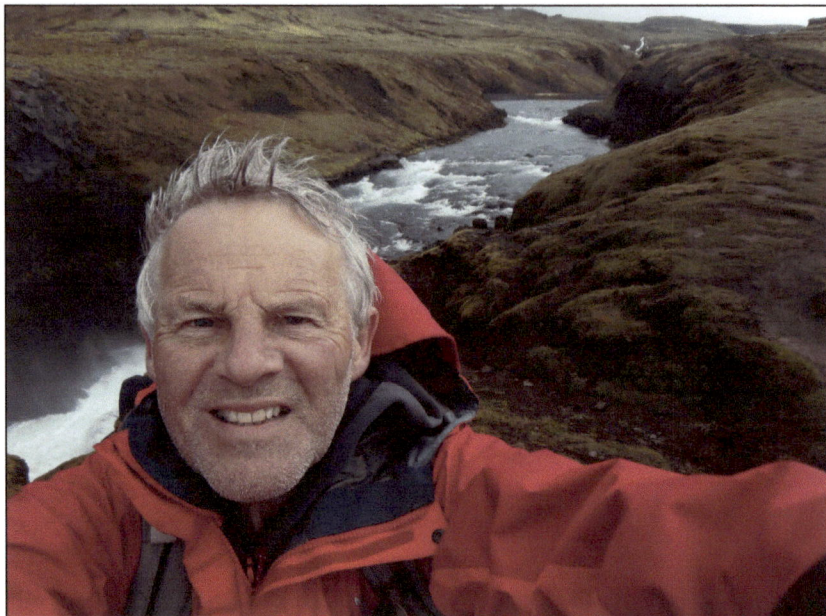

Nearing Skógar

was safe. She had been worried last night when I hadn't checked in and had rung Jonathan who had said I should take up dominoes. I took off my boots to dry in the wind and had lunch – the last of my vestiges of my bread, apple and cheese. I was so busy writing my journal that I missed my bus. It was blue, which I wasn't expecting. Maybe my ticket wouldn't have worked anyway. Four hours to wait, I thought. Nevermind. But a man had heard me asking about missing the bus in the hotel offered me a lift.

He was from Rhode Island and had been in the military 29 years. He now works in health and safety. He kindly drove me all the way to the Bus Hostel in Reykjavik where I was booked in a mixed 16-room dormitory.

The hostel was clean and well organised and fine for one night. I had a shower and a rest and called home, I set off about 7pm in search of a restaurant. I liked the look of the Loki Cafe beside the cathedral and after checking for alternatives around the block went back and ordered meat soup, trout pate on rye bread in the form of a cake slice, a delicious salad and, something new to me, rye ice cream. All with a large beer to top it off.

I walked down to the main street, the Laugavegur, named after the trail I

Tourists at the final falls on Skógar River

just done I presumed, and found a supermarket to buy biscuits for the office back in Cambridge. It was cold and drizzly so I went back to the hostel and chatted to an Aussie from Melbourne before making a cup of tea and getting to bed about 9.30. The place had filled up so I wondered how I'd sleep.

Reykjavik

Monday 19 June

In fact it wasn't too bad. A tall lithe blonde in black tights came in about 12.30 and swung almost noiselessly into the bunk above me. Her alarm went off at 3.30 and she swung out again equally effortlessly. I got up about 7.30 and did my things. I chatted a little in the kitchen. The other couple in the room with me are planning to do the trail and the girl asked advice. I told her there was a lot of snow and tried to give her an idea of the way without putting her off. I gathered my things bid goodbye to the friendly receptionist and started off the University where I left my suitcase in Rajesh's office.

Coffee at the Skógar Hotel

I crossed the motorway by a bridge and walked next to a wild area of ponds and brush – home of geese and sea birds. A Redshank strutted towards me emitting the same plaintive peeping I had heard on the walk. The geese had shat all over the path and I thought I would take a different way back with my wheeled case. Arctic tern swooped low over the water like they had over the Skógar River yesterday.

I found the office without difficulty and the key in the pigeon hole outside. I changed, repacked and set off dragging my case. I had just reached the main road when a car stopped and a man offered me a lift to the bus station. He said he done the Laugavegur trail with his twin sons when they were only six. I was impressed. He said they recovered quickly and played football each evening. He asked if I'd been with a group. You must be an experienced mountaineer then because that would have been a lot of snow. Yes, I said.

At the bus station I asked if they might refund part of my hiking bust passport. No, she said kindly. I thought not, I said. I need to get to the airport, I said, getting out my money. Here's a ticket for the Fly Bus instead, she said. How nice, I thought.

I went and had a coffee and another flapjack while I waited. I slept on the bus. The airport is the most efficient I've been in. This is a serious business for Iceland – processing tourists in such an efficient and welcoming way. I checked in my suitcase and found a place for soup with my last kroner. The flight was painless.

Meal at Loki Cafe. Beer, meat soup, trout pate, salad and rye ice cream

Note on logistics

I caught the 6.40am Reykjavik Excursions coach from the City Hostel in the north-east of the city and was able to start walking at 11am. There was a later bus at 8.30am from the BSI bus terminal. To return I was aiming for a 4.30pm Reykjavik Excursions bus from Skógar to Reykjavik. If I had missed this one, there was a later one at 9pm. The Hiking Bus Pass was about 12,000 króna.

I camped two nights, in Álftavatn and Emstrur, and stayed in the hut on the Fimmvörðuháls Pass one night. Camping cost 2,000 króna and the hut 6,500.

Three principles I follow in selecting what gear to take are: travel light, keep dry and comfortable boots. So the first thing is don't take things you don't need and what you do take keep as light as possible. I only broke this rule in terms of food. I generally prefer fresh food to processed and dried food, but this is generally heavier. My packed rucksack weighed 11.25 kilos, of which nearly 4 kilos were food and water, all of which I brought from the UK.

I had all I needed from many previous trips but I forgot to take gaiters and gloves. I decided I needed gaiters for the snow and to keep ash out of my boots and gloves because it was colder than I had imagined. I bought them at the outdoor Fjallakofinn at Laugavegur 11. In the event I needed the gaiters but not the gloves.

The gear performed well and I was comfortable, warm and dry. The tent lacked structure, having only one large hoop and three tiny fitted corners poles. I fixed extra guy ropes from cord I took with me and anchored these with rocks in case of high wind. There was heavy rain one night and the water pooled in the fly-sheet but it didn't leak being very high performance fabric. Nearly all the other campers had much heavier 4-season tents which would obviously perform better in more severe conditions. The Thermarest is well worth the extra weight. The Jetboil stove is fantastic, boiling water for a meal or a brew in just over a minute. I still had gas left from the tiny 100gm cannister after 4 days use.

I had winter weight Haglof walking trousers made from quick drying stretch Schoeller fabric. But I regretted not wearing my Gore-Tex Berghaus over-trousers in the last stretch over the Fimmvörðuháls Pass when it rained heavily.

Gear list

Gear	Item	Weight
Rucksac	Lightwave Fastpack 30 lt	963
Tent	Nordisk ultra lightweight Telemark 2	950
Sleeping bag	Rab 3 season in SeatoSummit 13L Dry sack	1600
Sleeping mat	Thermarest womens prolight	530
Cutlery	Plastic spoon and Gerber paraframe	40
Stove	Jetboil Zip with cannister and lighter	460
Food Containers	Assorted plastic bottles and bags	400
Compass	Silva mini	10
Headtorch	Petzi E-lite (unnecessary)	27
Map	Sérkort 4 Landmannalaugar 1:100,000	100
Guide	Zimmer, B (2014) The Laugavegur Trail	180
Notebook	Silveline memo book and pen, Ortleib waterproof bag	100
Washbag	Contact lenses, toothbrush/paste, deodorant, earplugs, mask	250
Camera	Olympus Stylus 16mp, 2 Duracell batteries, Lowepro case	250
Phone	iPhone 5SE	115
Reading glasses		20
Food		
Dried meals	3 meals Adventure Food; Travellund; Trek N' Eat	480
Loaf	Rye Sourdough	600
Butter		100
Cheese	2 Sainsbury Parmigiano Regianno	400
Apples	4 Pink Lady	700
Nuts	Almonds, brazil nuts, walnuts	200
Muesli	Oats and nuts	200
Dried milk		100
Tea	20 bags	40
Drinking chocolate		60
Chocolate	2 Black&Greens 75%	200
Water	500ml	500
Spare clothing		
Aqua shoes	Bluerush	400
Overtrousers	Berghaus	200
Duvet	Marmot sleeveless Stockholm vest, SeatoSummit 4L drysack	450
Gloves	Dakine storm liner	75
Vest	Arcterix long sleeved	150
Shirt	Arcterix zip neck	180
Underpants		40
Socks		60
Spectacles		80
Water bottle	Platypus soft bottle (empty)	10
TOTAL CARRIED		11,220
Clothing		
Boots	Meindl Bhutan	1600
Gaiters	SeatoSummit ankle	200
Anorak	Mountain Equipment Janek jacket red	515
Fleece	Berhaus BenOss windproof hooded	570
Trousers	Haglof	500
Belt		70
Underpants		45
Vest	Arcterix short sleeved	100
Socks		60
Poles	Leki Makalu	500
TOTAL WORN		4,160

Skogá River Canyon with wheeling Artic Tern

www.ingramcontent.com/pod-product-compliance
Lightning Source LLC
Chambersburg PA
CBHW041530090426
42738CB00035B/29